Alaskan Hats using Slip Stitch

Lori Adams

Introducing A Better Way To Crochet Cables

LEISURE ARTS, INC. • Maumelle, Arkansas

Slip Stitch Hats

Introducing A Better Way To Crochet Cables

Ben Adams Photography

This book is the result of my quest to find a better way to crochet cables. I've always loved how knitted cables look but have been disappointed in how they look when they've been crocheted, so over the years I've been obsessed with trying different things in an attempt to improve how they are made. It was during this quest that I started to realize how versatile the lowly slip stitch can be. The six different basic slip stitches can be arranged in endless combinations, and it was while experimenting with these combinations that magic started to happen! Beautiful designs, stretchy stitches, luxurious fabrics that had amazing drape, and smooth cables started to appear! The quest was over and I had fallen in love with slip stitching. The hats in this book are easy to make and so much fun to crochet that you'll want to make them for all of your friends and family. And then, you are going to fall in love with slip stitching too!

Lori Adams

CONTENTS

MEET LORI ADAMS

Lori Adams lives in Sitka, Alaska with her husband, Dale, who is a hunting guide. Together they raised 2 sons, Benjamin and Levi. Lori works as "camp cook" on their boat as they cruise the beautiful inland waters of Southeast Alaska with their clients. Although there is plenty of work to be done on board, there is also lots of time to crochet. "It's so peaceful and quiet when the boat is anchored up in a snug harbor and the hunters have gone ashore for the day. No phone calls, no emails or paperwork, no visitors, none of the normal hustle or bustle of home. Once my dishes and meal prep are done I can just sit in a quite corner and crochet with no distractions," Lori says. "I really feel that I do my best designing and get the most crocheting done when I am out on the boat. And the scenery is breathtaking! Sometimes inspiration for my next design is just right outside the window!"

Ben Adams Photography

Ben Adams lives in Sitka, Alaska with his wife, Emily, and their black lab, Kona. He is the son of Dale and Lori Adams and spent most of his childhood on the waters of Southeast Alaska, as the family made their livelihood commercial fishing, tendering, and guiding. Ben now works as a Salmon Biologist and continues to explore this remote wilderness that is his home. He truly enjoys all forms of outdoor recreation and subsistence living. Whether he is underwater, on the boat, up a river, or in the mountains, he never leaves the camera at home.

TIPS FOR SUCCESSFUL SLIP STITCHING

The key to successful slip stitching is loose tension! Loose tension is critical for achieving thin, soft, stretchy fabric that drapes well. Slip stitches are, by their very nature, really tight, so it takes special effort on the part of the crocheter to overcome this tendency and crochet large, loose stitches. The best way to achieve loose tension is to use a larger hook than you would normally use, but that is not always enough, so you'll need to adopt a technique that ensures that each stitch stays open more than usual. I'm right handed, so I find that my best technique is to kick up the butt end of my hook in an upward motion with my right hand while manipulating the work in a downward motion with my left hand for every stitch. If you struggle a lot to be able to push your hook through the spaces, have to use your fingernail to pull the loop down over your hook for every stitch, or hear the yarn squeaking when you crochet, your tension is too tight. The goal is to be able to work along at a good pace most of the time. Loose slip stitching takes practice, and the best way to practice is to start slip stitching!

Another challenge when slip stitching is being able to "read" your work and be able to figure out in which space and in which line of loops you should be working. This takes practice. Slip stitches have very little height which causes the rows to be compressed. The patterns in this book rarely call for slip stitching through both loops, so there are almost always numerous rows of loops running along the top of your work. The first and the last stitches of each row are definitely the hardest to identify, as they are often pulled down inside the work where you can't easily see them. If you are stuggling to read your work, you can insert a stitch marker in the top of the first and last stitch of each row and move it up with each row until you become more proficient. Keeping an accurate count of the stitches in each row is critical and will ensure that you haven't skipped any of these elusive stitches.

Finally, always turn your work in a clockwise direction at the end of each row *with the yarn behind the hook and out of the way unless the row begins with an inverse stitch.*

Six Types of Slip Stitches

Slip stitch: Insert hook through **both** loops from the **front** with the yarn **behind** the hook, YO and draw through all loops on hook.

Inverted slip stitch: Insert hook through **both** loops from **back** to **front** with the yarn in **front** of the hook, YO and draw through all loops on hook.

Slip stitch in Front Loop Only: Insert hook in Front Loop Only ***(Fig. 3, page 61)*** with the yarn **behind** the hook, YO and draw through all loops on hook.

Inverted slip stitch in Front Loop Only: Insert hook from **back** to **front** in Front Loop Only ***(Fig. 3, page 61)*** with the yarn in **front** of the hook, YO and draw through all loops on hook.

Slip stitch in Back Loop Only: Insert hook in Back Loop Only ***(Fig. 3, page 61)*** with the yarn **behind** the hook, YO and draw through all loops on hook.

Inverted slip stitch in Back Loop Only: Insert hook from **back** to **front** through Back Loop Only ***(Fig. 3, page 61)*** with the yarn in **front** of the hook, YO and draw through all loops on hook.

SIMPLE SLIP STITCH

EASY

Shopping List

Yarn

(Medium Weight) MEDIUM 4

[5 ounces, 250 yards

(141 grams, 228 meters)

per skein]:

- ☐ 1 skein

Crochet Hook

- ☐ Size K (6.5 mm)

  or size needed for gauge

Additional Supplies

- ☐ Locking stitch marker
- ☐ Yarn needle

SIZE INFORMATION

Fits head circumference:

Small - 14-17" (35.5-43 cm)

Medium - 17½-20" (44.5-51 cm)

Large - 20½-23" (52-58.5 cm)

Size Note: For ease in following the pattern, we have printed the instructions for each size in a different color:

size Small in Blue

size Medium in Pink

size Large in Green

Instructions in Black apply to all sizes.

GAUGE INFORMATION

14 sts and 20 rows = 3½" (9 cm)

Gauge Swatch: 3½" (9 cm) square

Ch 15 **tightly**, pull last ch completely closed.

Work same as Body for 20 rows.

Finish off.

BODY

Ch 36{41-46} **tightly**, pull last ch completely closed.

Row 1 (Right side)**:** Working in top loops of beginning ch ***(Fig. 1, page 61)***, slip st in second ch from hook and each ch across; ch 1, pull ch closed: 35{40-45} sts.

Note: Loop a short piece of yarn around any st to mark Row 1 as **right** side.

Rows 2 thru 73{85-93}: Turn; working in Back Loops Only ***(Fig. 3, page 61)***, slip st in each st across; ch 1, pull ch closed.

At end of last row, remove loop from hook and place on locking st marker.

Lay the rectangle flat with the st marker at the upper right corner and the tail of the foundation ch at the bottom right corner ***(Photo A, page 12)***.

The unstretched rectangle should measure 8¾" x 12¾" (22 cm x 32.5 cm) for size Small, 10" x 14¾" (25.5 cm x 37.5 cm) for size Medium and 11¼" x 16¼" (28.5 cm x 41.5 cm) for size Large. Add or subtract rows to achieve a perfect fit, ending by working a **right** side row.

FINISHING

SEAM

Fold the rectangle in half with the last row and beginning ch together ***(Photo B)***.

Remove marker and place loop on hook; insert opposite end of hook in free loop of first beginning ch ***(Photo C)***, draw loop through beginning ch ***(Photo D)***.

To finish the seam, ★ slip st **tightly** through **both** edges by inserting your hook first through bottom free loop of next ch and then through Back Loop Only of next slip st on last row, YO and draw through loops on hook; repeat from ★ across; finish off.

The side of the hat is now closed. Notice that when the hat is laying relaxed on the table, the seam is visible, but when you stretch the hat out a little bit the seam becomes invisible.

CLOSING TOP OF HAT

Designate the nicest edge as the bottom of the hat. Cut a strand of yarn 12" (30.5 cm) long. Thread yarn needle with strand and weave through loose loops along top edge ***(Photo E)***.

Gather tightly to close and secure ends. Attach pom-pom ***(Figs. 4a-c, page 63)*** if desired.

Photo A

Photo B

Photo C

Photo D

Photo E

Northern lights in the starry night sky.

BOBBLES HAT

EASY

Shopping List

Yarn

(Medium Weight) MEDIUM 4

[5 ounces, 256 yards

(141 grams, 234 meters) per skein]:

- ☐ 1 skein

Crochet Hook

- ☐ Size K (6.5 mm)

  or size needed for gauge

Additional Supplies

- ☐ Locking stitch marker
- ☐ Yarn needle
- ☐ Pom-pom (optional)

SIZE INFORMATION

Fits head circumference:

Small - 15-17½" (38-44.5 cm)

Medium - 18-20½" (45.5-52 cm)

Large - 21-23½" (53.5-59.5 cm)

Size Note: For ease in following the pattern, we have printed the instructions for each size in a different color:

size Small in Blue

size Medium in Pink

size Large in Green

Instructions in Black apply to all sizes.

GAUGE INFORMATION

14 sts and 20 rows = 3½" (9 cm)

Gauge Swatch: 3½" (9 cm) square

Ch 15 **tightly**, pull last ch completely closed.

Row 1 (Right side)**:** Working in top loops of beginning ch ***(Fig. 1, page 61)***, slip st in second ch from hook and each ch across; ch 1, pull ch closed: 14 sts.

Rows 2-20: Turn; working in Back Loops Only ***(Fig. 3, page 61)***, slip st in each st across; ch 1, pull ch closed.

Finish off.

STITCH GUIDE

TREBLE CROCHET *(abbreviated tr)*

YO twice, insert hook in st indicated, YO and pull up a loop (4 loops on hook), (YO and draw through 2 loops on hook) 3 times.

BODY

Ch 37{46-52} **tightly**, pull last ch completely closed.

Row 1 (Right side)**:** Working in top loops of beginning ch ***(Fig. 1, page 61)***, slip st in second ch from hook and in next 5 chs, ★ tr in next ch, push tr to **right** side **(now and throughout)**, slip st in next 5 chs; repeat from ★ 1{2-3} time(s) **more**, tr in next ch, slip st in last 17{20-20} chs; ch 1, pull ch closed: 36{45-51} sts.

Note: Loop a short piece of yarn around any st to mark Row 1 as **right** side.

Row 2 (WS)**:** Turn; working in Back Loops Only ***(Fig. 3, page 61)***, slip st in first 12{15-15} sts, inverted slip st in next 20{26-32} sts ***(See Six Types of Slip Sts, page 7)***, slip st in last 4 sts; ch 1, pull ch closed.

Row 3 (RS)**:** Turn; slip st in Back Loop Only of first 4 sts, ★ slip st in Front Loop Only of next 5 sts, tr in Front Loop Only of next st; repeat from ★ 2{3-4} times **more**, slip st in Front Loop Only of next 2 sts, slip st in Back Loop Only of last 12{15-15} sts; ch 1, pull ch closed.

Row 4 (WS)**:** Turn; working in Back Loops Only, slip st in first 12{15-15} sts, inverted slip st in next 20{26-32} sts, slip st in last 4 sts; ch 1, pull ch closed.

Row 5 (RS)**:** Turn; slip st in Back Loop Only of first 4 sts, slip st in Front Loop Only of next 2 sts, ★ tr in Front Loop Only of next st, slip st in Front Loop Only of next 5 sts; repeat from ★ 2{3-4} times **more**, slip st in Back Loop Only of last 12{15-15} sts; ch 1, pull ch closed.

Rows 6 thru 55{67-79}: Repeat Rows 2-5, 12{15-18} times; then repeat Rows 2 and 3 once **more**.

At end of last row, remove loop from hook and place on locking st marker.

Lay the rectangle flat with the st marker at the upper right corner and the tail of the foundation ch at the bottom right corner ***(Photo A)***.

At the widest points, the unstretched piece should measure 9" x 14" (23 cm x 35.5 cm) for size Small, 10" x 18" (25.5 cm x 45.5 cm) for size Medium and 11" x 20" (28 cm x 51 cm) for size Large. Add or subtract rows to achieve a perfect fit, ending by working Row 3.

FINISHING

SEAM

Fold the rectangle in half with **wrong** sides of working edge and beginning ch together ***(Photo B)*** and beginning ch on top.

Remove marker and place loop on hook; insert opposite end of hook in free loop of first beginning ch ***(Photo C)***, draw loop through beginning ch ***(Photo D)***.

To finish the seam, ★ slip st **tightly** through **both** edges by inserting your hook first through bottom free loops of next ch and then through Back Loop Only of next slip st on last row, YO and draw through all loops on hook; repeat from ★ 10{13-13} times **more**. Turn the hat **wrong** side out; † slip st **tightly** through **both** edges by inserting your hook through the Back Loop Only of next st on last row, then through free loops of beginning ch, YO and draw through loops on hook †; repeat from † to † across; finish off.

Photo A

Photo B

Make sure that the Bobbles line up and the edges are even at the cuff edge. If it is uneven by a stitch, you should rip back and adjust by a stitch at the beginning of the seam to make sure you come out even at the cuff.

Photo C

Photo D

Photo E

The side of the hat is now closed. Notice that when the hat is laying relaxed on a table the seam is visible, but when you stretch the hat out a little bit, the seam becomes invisible.

Round rocks on the beach.

CLOSING TOP OF HAT

Cut a 12" (30.5 cm) length of yarn. Thread yarn needle with end and weave through loose loops along top edge *(Photo E, page 18)*.

Gather tightly to close and secure ends. Attach pom-pom *(Figs. 4a-c, page 63)* if desired.

CHECKERED SLOUCH HAT

INTERMEDIATE

Shopping List

Yarn

(Medium Weight) MEDIUM 4

[5 ounces, 250 yards (141 grams, 228 meters) per skein]:

- ☐ 1{1-2} skein(s)

Crochet Hook

- ☐ Size J (6 mm)
  or size needed for gauge

Additional Supplies

- ☐ Locking stitch marker
- ☐ Yarn needle
- ☐ Pom-pom (optional)

SIZE INFORMATION

Fits head circumference:

Small - 15-17" (38-43 cm)

Medium - 17½-19½" (44.5-49.5 cm)

Large - 20-22" (51-56 cm)

Size Note: For ease in following the pattern we have printed the instructions for each size in a different color:

GAUGE INFORMATION

14 sts and 20 rows = 3½" (9 cm)

Gauge Swatch: 3½" (9 cm) square

Ch 15 **tightly**, pull last ch completely closed.

Row 1 (Right side): Working in top loops of beginning ch ***(Fig. 1, page 61)***, slip st in second ch from hook and each ch across; ch 1, pull ch closed: 14 sts.

Rows 2-20: Turn; working in Back Loops Only ***(Fig. 3, page 61)***, slip st in each st across; ch 1, pull ch closed.

Finish off.

BODY

Ch 43{52-58} **tightly**, pull last ch completely closed.

Row 1 (WS)**:** Working in top loops of beginning ch ***(Fig. 1, page 61)***, slip st in second ch from hook and in next 5 chs, inverted slip st in next 6 chs ***(See Six Types of Slip Sts, page 7)***, ★ slip st in next 6 chs, inverted slip st in next 6 chs; repeat from ★ 0{1-1} time(s) **more** ***(see Zeros, page 61)***, slip st in last 18{15-21} chs; ch 1, pull ch closed: 42{51-57} sts.

Row 2 (RS)**:** Turn; slip st in Back Loop Only of first 18{15-21} sts ***(Fig. 3, page 61)***, ★ slip st in Front Loop Only of next 6 sts, slip st in Back Loop Only of next 6 sts; repeat from ★ 1{2-2} time(s) **more**; ch 1, pull ch closed.

Row 3 (WS)**:** Turn; working in Back Loops Only, slip st in first 6 sts, inverted slip st in next 6 sts, ★ slip st in next 6 sts, inverted slip st in next 6 sts; repeat from ★ 0{1-1} time(s) **more**, slip st in last 18{15-21} sts; ch 1, pull ch closed.

Rows 4-6: Repeat Rows 2 and 3 once; then repeat Row 2 once **more**.

Row 7 (WS)**:** Turn; working in Back Loops Only, slip st in first 12 sts, inverted slip st in next 6 sts, ★ slip st in next 6 sts, inverted slip st in next 6 sts; repeat from ★ 0{0-1} time(s) **more**, slip st in last 12{21-15} sts; ch 1, pull ch closed.

Row 8 (RS)**:** Ch 1, turn; slip st in Back Loop Only of first 12{21-15} sts, slip st in Front Loop Only of next 6 sts, ★ slip st in Back Loop Only of next 6 sts, slip st in Front Loop Only of next 6 sts; repeat from ★ 0{0-1} time(s) **more**, slip st in Back Loop Only of last 12 sts; ch 1, pull ch closed.

Rows 9-12: Repeat Rows 7 and 8 twice.

Row 13 (WS)**:** Turn; working in Back Loops Only, slip st in first 6 sts, inverted slip st in next 6 sts, ★ slip st in next 6 sts, inverted slip st in next 6 sts; repeat from ★ 0{1-1} time(s) **more**, slip st in last 18{15-21} sts; ch 1, pull ch closed.

Rows 14 thru 71{83-95}: Repeat Rows 2-13, 4{5-6} times, then repeat Rows 2-11 once **more**.

At end of last row, remove loop from hook and place on locking st marker.

Rock that has been cracked and checked with time.

Lay the rectangle flat with the st marker at the upper right corner and the tail of the foundation ch at the bottom right corner. The unstretched rectangle should measure 10" x 14" (25.5 cm x 35.5 cm) for size Small, 12" x17" (30.5 cm x 43 cm) for size Medium and 14" x 20" (35.5 cm x 51 cm) for size Large. Add or subtract rows to achieve a perfect fit, ending by working Row 11.

FINISHING

See Finishing, page 62.

BOBBLES & RIDGES

EASY

Shopping List

Yarn

(Medium Weight) MEDIUM 4

[3½ ounces, 175 yards

(100 grams, 160 meters) per

skein]:

☐ 1{1-2} skein(s)

Crochet Hook

☐ Size K (6.5 mm)

or size needed for gauge

Additional Supplies

☐ Locking stitch marker

☐ Yarn needle

☐ Pom-pom (optional)

SIZE INFORMATION

Fits head circumference:

Small - 15½-17½" (39.5-44.5 cm)

Medium - 18-20" (45.5-51 cm)

Large - 20½-22½" (52-57 cm)

Size Note: For ease in following the pattern, we have printed the instructions for each size in a different color:

size Small in Blue

size Medium in Pink

size Large in Green

Instructions in Black apply to all sizes.

GAUGE INFORMATION

14 sts and 20 rows = 3½" (9 cm)

Gauge Swatch: 3½" (9 cm) square

Ch 15 **tightly**, pull last ch completely closed.

Row 1 (Right side)**:** Working in top loops of beginning ch ***(Fig. 1, page 61)***, slip st in second ch from hook and each ch across; ch 1, pull ch closed: 14 sts.

Rows 2-20: Turn; working in Back Loops Only ***(Fig. 3, page 61)***, slip st in each st across; ch 1, pull ch closed. Finish off.

STITCH GUIDE

BOBBLE (uses one st)

YO twice, insert hook in st indicated, YO and pull up a loop (4 loops on hook), (YO and draw through 2 loops on hook) twice (2 loops remaining on hook), insert hook in **same** st, YO and draw through st and through both loops on hook. Push Bobble to **right** side.

BODY

Sizes Small & Large Only

Ch 31{41} **tightly**, pull last ch completely closed.

Row 1 (Right side)**:** Working in top loops of beginning ch ***(Fig. 1, page 61)***, slip st in second ch from hook and in next 4 chs, ★ † sc in next ch, hdc in next ch, work Bobble in next ch, hdc in next ch, sc in next ch †, slip st in next 5 chs; repeat from ★ across to last 5 sts, then repeat from † to † once; ch 1, pull ch closed: 30{40} sts.

Note: Loop a short piece of yarn around any st to mark Row 1 as **right** side.

Row 2 (WS)**:** Turn; working in Back Loops Only *(Fig. 3, page 61)*, slip st in each st across; ch 1, pull ch closed.

Row 3 (RS)**:** Turn; working in Back Loops Only, slip st in first 10 sts, ★ sc in next st, hdc in next st, work Bobble in next st, hdc in next st, sc in next st, slip st in next 5 sts; repeat from ★ across; ch 1, pull ch closed.

Row 4 (WS)**:** Turn; slip st in Back Loop Only of each st across; ch 1, pull ch closed.

Row 5 (RS)**:** Turn; working in Back Loops Only, slip st in first 5 sts, ★ † sc in next st, hdc in next st, work Bobble in next st, hdc in next st, sc in next st †, slip st in next 5 sts; repeat from ★ across to last 5 sts, then repeat from † to † once; ch 1, pull ch closed.

Rows 6 thru 63{87}: Repeat Rows 2-5, 14{20} times; then repeat Rows 2 and 3 once **more**.

At end of last row, remove loop from hook and place on locking st marker.

Size Medium Only

Ch 36, **tightly**, pull the last ch completely closed.

Row 1 (Right side)**:** Working in top loops of beginning ch *(Fig. 1, page 61)*, slip st in second ch from hook and in next 4 chs, ★ sc in next ch, hdc in next ch, work Bobble in next ch, hdc in next ch, sc in next ch, slip st in next 5 chs; repeat from ★ across; ch 1, pull ch closed: 35 sts.

Note: Loop a short piece of yarn around any st to mark Row 1 as **right** side.

Row 2 (WS)**:** Turn; working in Back Loops Only *(Fig. 3, page 61)*, slip st in each st across; ch 1, pull ch closed.

Row 3 (RS)**:** Turn; working in Back Loops Only, slip st in first 10 sts, ★ † sc in next st, hdc in next st, work Bobble in next st, hdc in next st, sc in next st †, slip st in next 5 sts; repeat from ★ across to last 5 sts, then repeat from † to † once; ch 1, pull ch closed.

Row 4 (WS)**:** Turn; slip st in Back Loop Only of each st across; ch 1, pull ch closed.

Row 5 (RS)**:** Ch 1, turn; working in Back Loops Only, slip st in first 5 sts, ★ sc in next st, hdc in next st, work Bobble in next st, hdc in next st, sc in next st, slip st in next 5 sts; repeat from ★ across; ch 1, pull ch closed.

Rows 6-75: Repeat Rows 2-5, 17 times; then repeat Rows 2 and 3 once **more**.

At end of last row, remove loop from hook and place on locking st marker.

Light reflecting on the water.

The unstretched rectangle should measure 8" x 13" (20.5 cm x 33 cm) for size Small, 9¾" x 17" (25 cm x 43 cm) for size Medium and 10¾" x 20" (27.5 cm x 51 cm) for size Large. Add or subtract rows to achieve a perfect fit, ending by working Row 3.

FINISHING

See Finishing, page 62.

BASIC CABLES

INTERMEDIATE

Shopping List

Yarn

(Medium Weight) MEDIUM 4

[5 ounces, 256 yards (141 grams, 234 meters) per skein]:

- ☐ 1{1-2} skein(s)

Crochet Hook

- ☐ Size K (6.5 mm) **or** size needed for gauge

Additional Supplies

- ☐ Locking stitch markers - 3 Color A and 3 Color B
- ☐ Yarn needle
- ☐ Pom-pom (optional)

SIZE INFORMATION

Fits head circumference:

Small - 16-19" (40.5-48.5 cm)

Medium - 19½-22" (49.5-56 cm)

Large - 22½-25" (57-63.5 cm)

Size Note: For ease in following the pattern, we have printed the instructions for each size in a different color:

size Small in Blue

size Medium in Pink

size Large in Green

Instructions in Black apply to all sizes.

GAUGE INFORMATION

14 sts and 20 rows = 3½" (9 cm)

Gauge Swatch: 3½" (9 cm) square

Ch 15 **tightly**, pull last ch completely closed.

Row 1 (Right side)**:** Working in top loops of beginning ch ***(Fig. 1, page 61)***, slip st in second ch from hook and each ch across; ch 1, pull ch closed: 14 sts.

Rows 2-20: Turn; working in Back Loops Only ***(Fig. 3, page 61)***, slip st in each st across; ch 1, pull ch closed. Finish off.

CABLE STRIP

CUFF

Ch 34{43-47} **tightly**, and pull last ch completely closed.

Row 1 (RS)**:** Slip st in top loop ***(Fig. 1, page 61)*** of second ch from hook and in next 9{14-14} chs; ch 1, insert Color A marker in front loop of ch just made: 10{15-15} slip sts.

Row 2 (WS)**:** Turn; working in Back Loops Only ***(Fig. 3, page 61)***, slip st in each st across; ch 1, pull ch closed.

UNIT 1

Row 3 (RS)**:** Turn; slip st in Back Loop Only of first 10{15-15} sts, ch 1, push marker to **wrong** side; working in beginning ch, slip st in top loop only of next 4 chs; ch 1, insert Color A marker in front loop of ch just made: 14{19-19} slip sts and 1 ch.

Row 4 (WS)**:** Turn; working in Back Loops Only, slip st in next 4 sts, slip st in next ch and in last 10{15-15} sts; ch 1, pull ch closed: 15{20-20} slip sts.

UNIT 2

Row 5 (RS)**:** Turn; slip st in Back Loop Only of first 15{20-20} sts, ch 1, push marker to **wrong** side; working in beginning ch, slip st in top loop only of next 4 chs; ch 1, insert Color A marker in front loop of ch just made: 19{24-24} slip sts and 1 ch.

Row 6 (WS)**:** Turn; working in Back Loops Only, slip st in next 4 sts, slip st in next ch and in next 5 sts, working in **front** of previous rows, slip st in Color A marked loop below, do **not** remove marker: 11 slip sts.

Row 7 (RS)**:** Turn; skip first st, working in Back Loops Only, slip st in next 10 sts; ch 1, insert Color B marker in front loop of ch just made: 10 slip sts.

Row 8 (WS)**:** Turn; working in Back Loops Only, slip st in next 10 sts, slip st again in Color A marked loop below, remove marker: 11 slip sts.

UNIT 3

Row 9 (RS)**:** Turn; skip first st, working in Back Loops Only, slip st in next 10 sts, ch 1, push markers to **wrong** side; working in beginning ch, slip st in top loop only of next 4 chs; ch 1, insert Color A marker in front loop of ch just made: 14 slip sts and 1 ch.

Row 10 (WS)**:** Turn; working in Back Loops Only, slip st in next 4 sts, slip st in next ch and in next 5 sts; working in **front** of previous rows, slip st in Color A marked loop below, do **not** remove marker: 11 slip sts.

Row 11 (RS)**:** Turn; skip first st, working in Back Loops Only, slip st in next 10 sts; ch 1, insert Color B marker in front loop of ch just made: 10 slip sts.

Row 12 (WS)**:** Turn; working in Back Loops Only, slip st in next 10 sts, slip st again in Color A marked loop below, remove marker: 11 slip sts.

UNIT 4

Row 13 (RS)**:** Turn; skip first st, working in Back Loops Only, slip st in next 10 sts, ch 1, push markers to **wrong** side; working in beginning ch, slip st in top loop only of next 4 chs; ch 1, insert Color A marker in front loop of ch just made: 14 slip sts and 1 ch.

Row 14 (WS)**:** Turn; working in Back Loops Only, slip st in next 4 sts, slip st in next ch and in next 5 sts; working in **front** of previous rows, slip st in Color A marked loop below, remove marker: 11 slip sts.

Row 15 (RS)**:** Turn; skip first st, working in Back Loops Only, slip st in next 10 sts; ch 1, insert Color B marker in front loop of ch just made: 10 slip sts.

Row 16 (WS)**:** Turn; slip st in Back Loop Only of first 10 sts, working in **front** of previous rows, slip st in Color B marked loop below, remove marker.

NEXT 1{2-3} UNIT(S)

Rows 17 thru 20{24-28}: Repeat Rows 13-16, 1{2-3} time(s).

LAST UNIT

Row 21{25-29} (RS)**:** Turn; skip first st, working in Back Loops Only, slip st in next 10 sts, ch 1, push markers to **wrong** side; working in beginning ch, slip st in top loop only of next 3 chs; ch 1, pull ch closed: 13 slip sts and 1 ch.

Row 22{26-30} (WS)**:** Turn; working in Back Loops Only, slip st in first 3 sts, slip st in next ch and in next 5 sts; working in **front** of previous rows, insert hook in Color A marked loop below, then insert hook in Color B marked loop below, YO and draw through all loops on hook, remove markers: 10 slip sts.

Row 23{27-31} (RS)**:** Turn; skip first st, working in Back Loops Only, slip st in next 9 sts; ch 1, pull ch closed: 9 slip sts.

Row 24{28-32} (WS)**:** Turn; working in Back Loops Only, slip st in first 4 sts; working in **front** of previous rows, insert hook in Color A marked loop below, then insert hook in Color B marked loop below, YO and draw through all loops on hook, remove markers: 5 slip sts.

Row 25{29-33} (RS)**:** Turn; skip first st, working in Back Loops Only, slip st in next 4 sts; ch 1, pull ch closed: 4 slip sts.

If you count the sts across the tops of the cuff and all Units you should have a total of 39{49-54} available sts. If you have made a mistake somewhere in the cable and you have a few more or less, don't tear it all out. You can skip or add a few sts in the next row to make up for it and it won't show.

Row 26{30-34} (WS)**:** Turn; working in Back Loops Only, slip st in first 3 sts, skip next st on Last Unit, ★ skip first st on **next** Unit, slip st in next 4 sts; repeat from ★ 4{5-6} times **more**, slip st in last 10{15-15} sts; ch 1, pull ch closed: 33{42-46} slip sts.

Coils of rope on the deck.

DIVIDER ROWS

Row 27{31-35} (RS)**:** Turn; working in Back Loops Only, slip st in first 10{15-15} sts, sc in next 20{24-28} sts, slip st in last 3 sts; ch 1, pull ch closed: 20{24-28} sc and 13{18-18} slip sts.

Row 28{32-36} (WS)**:** Turn; working in Back Loops Only, slip st in each st across; ch 1, pull ch closed: 33{42-46} slip sts.

One Cable Strip complete.

Row 29{33-37} (RS)**:** Turn; slip st in Back Loop Only of first 10{15-15} sts; ch 1, insert Color A marker in front loop of ch just made.

Repeat Rows 2 thru 29{33-37}, 6{8-10} times; then repeat Rows 2 thru 27{31-35} once **more**: 8{10-12} Cable Strips complete.

At end of last row, remove loop from hook and place on locking st marker.

Lay the rectangle flat with **wrong** side facing and the st marker at the upper right corner.

The unstretched rectangle should measure 9¼" x 13½" (23.5 cm x 34.5 cm) for size Small, 11" x 16½" (28 cm x 42 cm) for size Medium and 13" x 20" (33 cm x 51 cm) for size Large. Add or subtract rows to achieve a perfect fit, ending by working Row 27{31-35}.

FINISHING

See Finishing, page 62.

CABLES & BOBBLES

INTERMEDIATE

Shopping List

Yarn

(Medium Weight) MEDIUM 4

[5 ounces, 256 yards (141 grams, 234 meters) per skein]:

- ☐ 1{1-2} skein(s)

Crochet Hook

- ☐ Size K (6.5 mm)
  or size needed for gauge

Additional Supplies

- ☐ Locking stitch markers - 3 Color A and 3 Color B
- ☐ Yarn needle
- ☐ Pom-pom (optional)

SIZE INFORMATION

Fits head circumference:

Small - 15-17½" (38-44.5 cm)

Medium - 18-20½" (45.5-52 cm)

Large - 21-23½" (53.5-59.5 cm)

Size Note: For ease in following the pattern, we have printed the instructions for each size in a different color:

size Small in Blue

size Medium in Pink

size Large in Green

Instructions in Black apply to all sizes.

GAUGE INFORMATION

14 sts and 20 rows = 3½" (9 cm)

Gauge Swatch: 3½" (9 cm) square

Ch 15 **tightly**, pull last ch completely closed.

Row 1 (Right side)**:** Working in top loops of beginning ch ***(Fig. 1, page 61)***, slip st in second ch from hook and each ch across; ch 1, pull ch closed: 14 sts.

Rows 2-20: Turn; working in Back Loops Only ***(Fig. 3, page 61)***, slip st in each st across; ch 1, pull ch closed.

Finish off.

STITCH GUIDE

BOBBLE (uses one st)

YO twice, insert hook in st indicated, YO and pull up a loop (4 loops on hook), (YO and draw through 2 loops on hook) twice (2 loops remaining on hook), insert hook in **same** st, YO and draw through st and through both loops on hook. Push Bobble to **right** side.

CABLE/BOBBLE STRIP

Bobble Strip

Ch 35{43-48} **tightly**, pull last ch completely closed.

Row 1 (RS)**:** Working in top loops of beginning ch ***(Fig. 1, page 61)***, slip st in second ch from hook and in next 9{14-14} chs (cuff), sc in next ch, hdc in next ch, work Bobble in next ch, hdc in next ch, sc in next ch, ★ slip st in next 3 chs, sc in next ch, hdc in next ch, work Bobble in next ch, hdc in next ch, sc in next ch; repeat from ★ 1{1-2} time(s) **more**, slip st in last 3{6-3} chs; ch 1, pull ch closed: 34{42-47} sts.

Rows 2 and 3: Turn; working in Back Loops Only ***(Fig. 3, page 61)***, slip st in each st across; ch 1, pull ch closed.

Row 4 (Foundation Row - WS)**:** Turn; working in Back Loops Only, inverted slip st in first 24{27-32} sts ***(see Six Types of Slip Stitches, page 7)***, slip st in last 10{15-15} sts; ch 1, pull ch closed.

Cable Strip

CUFF

Row 5 (RS)**:** Turn; working in Back Loops Only, slip st in first 10{15-15} sts; ch 1, insert Color A marker in front loop of ch just made.

Row 6 (WS)**:** Turn; working in Back Loops Only, slip st in each st across; ch 1, pull ch closed.

UNIT 1

Row 7 (RS)**:** Turn; slip st in Back Loop Only first 10{15-15} sts, ch 1, push marker to **wrong** side; working in sts on Foundation Row, slip st in Front Loop Only of next 4 sts; ch 1, insert Color A marker in front loop of ch just made: 14{19-19} slip sts and 1 ch.

Row 8 (WS)**:** Turn; working in Back Loops Only, slip st in next 4 sts, slip st in next ch and in last 10{15-15} sts; ch 1, pull ch closed: 15{20-20} slip sts.

UNIT 2

Row 9 (RS)**:** Turn; slip st in Back Loop Only of first 15{20-20} sts, ch 1, push marker to **wrong** side; working in sts on Foundation Row, slip st in Front Loop Only of next 4 sts; ch 1, insert Color A marker in front loop of ch just made: 19{24-24} slip sts and 1 ch.

Row 10 (WS)**:** Turn; working in Back Loops Only, slip st in next 4 sts, slip st in next ch and in next 5 sts, working in **front** of previous rows, slip st in Color A marked loop below, do **not** remove marker: 11 slip sts.

Row 11 (RS)**:** Turn; skip first st, working in Back Loops Only, slip st in next 10 sts; ch 1, insert Color B marker in front loop of ch just made: 10 slip sts.

Row 12 (WS)**:** Turn; working in Back Loops Only, slip st in next 10 sts, slip st again in Color A marked loop below, remove marker: 11 slip sts.

UNIT 3

Row 13 (RS)**:** Turn; skip first st, slip st in Back Loop Only of next 10 sts, ch 1, push markers to **wrong** side; working in sts on Foundation Row, slip st in Front Loop Only of next 4 sts; ch 1, insert Color A marker in front loop of ch just made: 14 slip sts and 1 ch.

Row 14 (WS)**:** Turn; working in Back Loops Only, slip st in next 4 sts, slip st in next ch and in next 5 sts; working in **front** of previous rows, slip st in Color A marked loop below, do **not** remove marker: 11 slip sts.

Row 15 (RS)**:** Turn; skip first st, working in Back Loops Only, slip st in next 10 sts; ch 1, insert Color B marker in front loop of ch just made: 10 slip sts.

Row 16 (WS)**:** Turn; working in Back Loops Only, slip st in next 10 sts, slip st again in Color A marked loop below, remove marker: 11 slip sts.

UNIT 4

Row 17 (RS)**:** Turn; skip first st, slip st in Back Loop Only of next 10 sts, ch 1, push markers to **wrong** side; working in sts on Foundation Row, slip st in Front Loop Only of next 4 sts; ch 1, insert Color A marker in front loop of ch just made: 14 slip sts and 1 ch.

Row 18 (WS)**:** Turn; working in Back Loops Only, slip st in next 4 sts, slip st in next ch and in next 5 sts; working in **front** of previous rows, slip st in Color A marked loop below, remove marker: 11 slip sts.

Row 19 (RS)**:** Turn; skip first st, working in Back Loops Only, slip st in next 10 sts; ch 1, insert Color B marker in front loop of ch just made: 10 slip sts.

Row 20 (WS)**:** Turn; working in Back Loops Only, slip st in next 10 sts, working in **front** of previous rows, slip st in Color B marked loop below, remove marker.

NEXT 1{2-3} UNIT(S)

Rows 21 thru 24{28-32}: Repeat Rows 17-20,1{2-3} time(s).

LAST UNIT

Row 25{29-33} (RS)**:** Turn; skip first st, slip st in Back Loop Only of next 10 sts, ch 1, push markers to **wrong** side; working in sts on Foundation Row, slip st in Front Loop Only of next 4{3-4} sts; ch 1, pull ch closed: 14{13-14} slip sts and 1 ch.

Row 26{30-34} (WS)**:** Turn; working in Back Loops Only, slip st in next 4{3-4} sts, slip st in next ch and in next 5 sts; working in **front** of previous rows, insert hook in Color A marked loop below, then insert hook in Color B marked loop below, YO and draw through all loops on hook, remove markers: 11{10-11} slip sts.

Row 27{31-35} (RS)**:** Turn; skip first st, working in Back Loops Only, slip st in next 10{9-10} sts; ch 1, pull ch closed: 10{9-10} slip sts.

Row 28{32-36} (WS)**:** Turn; slip st in Back Loop Only of first 5{4-5} sts; working in **front** of previous rows, insert hook in Color A marked loop below, then insert hook in Color B marked loop, YO and draw through all loops on hook, remove markers: 6{5-6} slip sts.

Row 29{33-37} (RS)**:** Turn; skip first st, slip st in Back Loop Only of next 5{4-5} sts; ch 1, pull ch closed: 5{4-5} slip sts.

If you count the sts across the tops of the cuff and all Units you should have a total of 40{49-55} available sts. If you have made a mistake somewhere in the cable and you have a few more or less, don't tear it all out. You can skip or add a few sts in the next row to make up for it and it won't show.

Row 30{34-38} (WS)**:** Turn; working in Back Loops Only, inverted slip st in first 4{3-4} sts, skip next st on Last Unit, ★ skip first st on next Unit, inverted slip st in next 4 sts; repeat from ★ 4{5-6} times **more**, slip st in last 10{15-15} sts; ch 1, pull ch closed: 34{42-47} sts.

Row 31{35-39} (RS)**:** Turn; slip st in Back Loop Only of next 10{15-15} sts, slip st in Front Loop Only of each st across; ch 1, pull ch closed.

Row 32{36-40} (WS)**:** Turn; working in Back Loops Only, slip st in each st across; ch 1, pull ch closed.

One Cable/Bobble Strip complete.

Row 33{37-41} (RS)**:** Turn; working in Back Loops Only, slip st in first 10{15-15} sts, sc in next st, hdc in next st, work Bobble in next st, hdc in next st, sc in next st, ★ slip st in next 3 sts, sc in next st, hdc in next st, work Bobble in next st, hdc in next st, sc in next st; repeat from ★ 1{1-2} time(s) **more**, slip st in last 3{6-3} chs; ch 1, pull ch closed.

Ben Adams Photography

Ancient bear trail through the woods.

Repeat Rows 2 thru 33{37-41}, 4{5-6} times; then repeat Rows 2 thru 31{35-39} once **more**: 6{7-8} Cable/Bobble Strips complete.

At end of last row, remove loop from hook and place on locking st marker.

The unstretched rectangle should measure 9" x 14" (23 cm x 35.5 cm) for size Small, 11" x 17" (28 cm x 43 cm) for size Medium and 13" x 20" (33 cm x 51 cm) for size Large. The longer side of the rectangle should measure 1-2" (2.5-5 cm) less than desired head circumference. Add or subtract rows to achieve perfect fit, ending by working Row 31{35-39}.

FINISHING

See Finishing, page 62.

CABLES IN THE ROUND

INTERMEDIATE

Shopping List

Yarn

(Medium Weight) MEDIUM 4

[4 ounces, 203 yards (113 grams, 186 meters) per skein]:

- ☐ 1{1-2} skein(s)

Crochet Hook

- ☐ Size K (6.5 mm) **or** size needed for gauge

Additional Supplies

- ☐ Locking stitch markers - 5 Color A and 5 Color B
- ☐ Yarn needle
- ☐ Pom-pom (optional)

SIZE INFORMATION

Fits head circumference:

Small - 16-17" (40.5-43 cm)

Medium - 17½-19" (44.5-48.5 cm)

Large - 19½-21" (49.5-53.5 cm)

Size Note: For ease in following the pattern, we have printed the instructions for each size in a different color:

size Small in Blue

size Medium in Pink

size Large in Green

Instructions in Black apply to all sizes.

GAUGE INFORMATION

14 sts and 20 rows = 3½" (9 cm)

Gauge Swatch: 3½" (9 cm) square

Ch 15 **tightly**, pull last ch completely closed.

Row 1 (Right side)**:** Working in top loops of beginning ch ***(Fig. 1, page 61)***, slip st in second ch from hook and each ch across; ch 1, pull ch closed: 14 sts.

Rows 2-20: Turn; working in Back Loops Only ***(Fig. 3, page 61)***, slip st in each st across; ch 1, pull ch closed.

Finish off.

STITCH GUIDE

DECREASE

Insert hook in Back Loop Only of each of next 2 sts, YO and draw through all 3 loops on hook ***(counts as slip st)***.

HAT

RIBBING

Ch 13{16-19} **tightly**, pull last ch completely closed.

Row 1 (Right side)**:** Working in top loops of beginning ch ***(Fig. 1, page 61)***, slip st in second ch from hook and each ch across; ch 1, pull ch closed: 12{15-18} sts.

Note: Loop a short piece of yarn around any st to mark Row 1 as **right** side.

Rows 2 thru 63{85-105}: Turn; working in Back Loops Only ***(Fig. 3, page 61)***, slip st in each st across; ch 1, pull ch closed.

At end of last row, remove loop from hook and place on locking st marker.

Lay the rectangle flat with the st marker at the upper right corner and the tail of the foundation ch at the bottom right corner ***(Photo A)***.

The unstretched rectangle should measure 3" x 15" (7.5 cm x 38 cm) for size Small, 3½" x 16" (9 cm x 40.5 cm) for size Medium and 3¾" x 18" (9.5 cm x 45.5 cm) for size Large. The long side of the rectangle should measure 1-2" (2.5-5 cm) less than desired head circumference.

Fold the rectangle in half with the last row and beginning ch together ***(Photo B)***. Remove marker and place loop on hook, then push the other end of your hook under free loop of first beginning ch ***(Photo C)***, YO and draw through beginning ch ***(Photo D)***.

Photo A

Photo B

Photo C

Photo D

Photo E

Photo F

Photo G

Joining Row: ★ Slip st **tightly** through **both** edges, inserting hook through bottom loop of next beginning ch *(Fig. 2, page 61)* **and** through Back Loop Only of next slip st on last row, YO and draw through all loops on hook; repeat from ★ across; ch 1, pull ch closed; remove loop from hook and place on st marker; do **not** cut yarn.

Fold Ribbing in half, matching end of rows *(Photo E, page 47)*.

It can be a bit tricky to line up the edges perfectly, so it may be helpful to insert a marker on each edge to help guide you. You will see a single loop at each end of every other row around ribbing. Place a marker in one edge, then follow the line of stitches and mark the corresponding loop at the opposite edge *(Photo F, page 47)*.

Foundation Rnd: Place loop on hook; working in single loops on **both** edges, sc in first loops *(Photo G, page 47)*, 2 sc in next loops, ★ sc in next loops, 2 sc in next loops; repeat from ★ around to last 0{1-1} loop(s) *(See Zeros, page 61)*, 0{1-2} sc in last loop; join with slip st to first sc: 48{64-80} sc.

CABLE STRIP

CABLE UNIT 1

Row 1 (RS)**:** Slip st in Back Loop Only of next sc, ch 6, skip next 3 sc, slip st in Front Loop Only of next 4 sc; ch 1, insert Color A marker in front loop of ch just made: 5 slip sts and 1 ch-6 sp.

Row 2 (WS)**:** Turn; working in Back Loops Only, slip st in first 4 sts and in next 6 chs; ch 1, insert Color A marker in front loop of ch just made: 10 slip sts.

Row 3 (RS)**:** Turn; slip st in Back Loop Only of first 10 sts; ch 1, insert Color B marker in front loop of ch just made.

Row 4 (WS)**:** Turn; slip st in Back Loop Only of first 10 sts; ch 1, insert Color B marker in front loop of ch just made.

CABLE UNIT 2

Row 5 (RS)**:** Slip st in Back Loop Only of first 10 sts, ch 1, push markers to **wrong** side; working in sts on Foundation Rnd, slip st in Front Loop Only of next 4 sc; ch 1, insert Color A marker in front loop of ch just made: 14 slip sts and 1 ch.

Row 6 (WS)**:** Turn; working in Back Loops Only, slip st in first 4 sts, slip st in next ch and in next 5 sts; ch 1, insert Color A marker in front loop of ch just made: 10 slip sts.

Row 7 (RS)**:** Turn; slip st in Back Loop Only of first 10 sts; ch 1, insert Color B marker in front loop of ch just made.

Row 8 (WS)**:** Turn; slip st in Back Loop Only of first 10 sts; ch 1, insert Color B marker in front loop of ch just made.

CABLE UNIT 3

Row 9 (RS)**:** Turn; slip st in Back Loop Only of first 10 sts, ch 1, push markers to **wrong** side; working in sts on Foundation Rnd, slip st in Front Loop Only of next 4 sc; ch 1, insert Color A marker in front loop of ch just made: 14 sts and 1 ch.

Row 10 (WS)**:** Turn; working in Back Loops Only, slip st in first 4 sts, slip st in next ch and in next 5 sts; working in **front** of previous rows, slip st in Color A marked loop below, remove marker: 11 slip sts.

Row 11 (RS)**:** Turn; skip first st, slip st in Back Loops Only of next 10 sts; ch 1, insert Color B marker in front loop of ch just made.

Row 12 (WS)**:** Turn; working in Back Loops Only, slip st in first 10 sts; working in **front** of previous rows, slip st in Color B marked loop below, remove marker: 11 slip sts.

CABLE UNITS 4 THRU 10{14-18}

Rows 13 thru 40{56-72}: Repeat Rows 9-12, 7{11-15} times: 10{14-18} Cable Units complete.

CABLE UNIT 11{15-19}

Row 41{57-73} (RS)**:** Turn; slip st in Back Loop Only of first 10 sts, ch 1, push markers to **wrong** side; working in sts on Foundation Rnd, slip st in

Front Loop Only of last 4 sc; slip st in next Color A marked loop, remove marker: 14 sts and 1 ch.

Row 42{58-74} (WS)**:** Turn; working in Back Loops Only, slip st in next 4 sts, slip st in next ch and in next 5 sts; working in **front** of previous rows, slip st in Color A marked loop, remove marker: 11 slip sts.

Row 43{59-75} (RS)**:** Turn; skip first st, slip st in Back Loop Only of next 10 sts; slip st in next Color B marked loop, remove marker.

Row 44{60-76} (WS)**:** Turn; working in Back Loops Only, slip st in next 10 sts; working in **front** of previous rows, slip st in Color B marked loop below, remove marker: 11{15-19} Cable Units complete.

LAST CABLE UNIT

Row 45{61-77} (RS)**:** Turn; skip first st, slip st in Back Loop Only of next 10 sts, ch 1, working in **front** of previous rows, slip st in Front Loop Only of next st (same st as first st of Row 1) and in next 3 sts, pull Color A marked loop under first Cable Unit to **front** and slip st in marked loop, remove marker: 15 slip sts and 1 ch.

Row 46{62-78} (WS)**:** Turn; skip first st, slip st in Back Loop Only of next 4 sts, slip st in next ch and in next 5 sts; working in **front** of previous rows, slip st in Color A marked loop below, remove marker: 11 slip sts.

Row 47{63-79} (RS)**:** Turn; skip first st, slip st in Back Loop Only of next 10 sts, pull Color B marked loop under first Cable to **front** and slip st in marked loop, remove marker: 11 slip sts.

Row 48{64-80} (WS)**:** Turn; skip first st, slip st in Back Loop Only of next 10 sts; working in **front** of previous rows, slip st in Color B marked loop below, remove marker: 11 slip sts.

Row 49{65-81} (RS)**:** Turn; skip first st, slip st in Back Loop Only of next 4 sts: 12{16-20} Cable Units complete.

RIBBING BAND

The sts across the top of each cable unit are the new Foundation Rnd. If you have made a mistake somewhere in the cable, don't tear it out. You can skip or add a few sts in the next round to make up for it and it won't really show. The front loop of the first st on top of each cable can be very difficult to identify. It tends to get buried by the stitches around it. Sometimes it helps to look at the fifth sp on the left of each cable, isolate the correct working line of sps, then run your eye along that line to the right to find the first st in the cable. If that doesn't work, try looking at it from the wrong side. Once you find it, use a small crochet hook or the tip of a marker to pull it up so you can work in it.

Foundation Rnd: ★ Slip st in Front Loop Only of first 4 sts on **next** Cable Unit, skip next st on **same** Cable Unit; repeat from ★ around; join with slip st to Back Loop Only of first st: 48{64-80} slip sts.

Row 1: Ch 3{3-4}, pull last ch closed, slip st in top loop of second ch from hook and in next 1{1-2} ch(s), slip st in Back Loop Only of same st as joining on Foundation Rnd: 3{3-4} sts.

Row 2 (WS)**:** Turn; skip first st, slip st in Back Loop Only of last 2{2-3} sts; ch 1, pull ch closed.

Row 3 (RS)**:** Turn; working in Back Loops Only, slip st in first 2{2-3} sts and in next st on Foundation Rnd: 3{3-4} sts.

Rows 4 thru 95{127-159}: Repeat Rows 2 and 3, 46{62-78} times.

Row 96 (Joining Row)**:** Turn; skip first st on last row, matching **right** sides of beginning ch and last row, insert hook in free loop of first beginning ch and in Back Loop Only of next st on last row, YO and draw through all loops on hook, ★ insert hook in next free loop of beginning ch and in Back Loop Only of last st on last row, YO and draw through all loops on hook; repeat from ★ 0{0-1} time(s) more; do **not** finish off.

SECOND CABLE BAND

Foundation Rnd: Working in single loops on edge of Ribbing Band, slip st in each loop around; join with slip st to first st: 48{64-80} sts.

Repeat Rows 1 thru 49{63-81} of Cable Strip, working in slip sts where instructed to work in sc.

Sizes Medium & Large Only

Repeat Ribbing Band and Second Cable Band.

LAST RIBBING BAND

All Sizes

Foundation Rnd: ★ Working in Front Loops Only, slip st in first st on **next** Cable Unit, decrease, slip st in next st, skip next st on **same** Cable Unit; repeat from ★ around; join with slip st to Back Loop Only of first st: 36{48-60} slip sts.

Row 1: Ch 7{7-11}, pull last ch closed, slip st in top loop of second ch from hook and in next 5{5-9} chs, slip st in Back Loop Only of same st as joining on Foundation Rnd: 7{7-11} sts.

Row 2 (WS)**:** Turn; skip first st, slip st in Back Loop Only of last 6{6-10} sts; ch 1, pull ch closed.

Row 3 (RS)**:** Turn; working in Back Loops Only, slip st in first 6{6-10} sts and in next st on Foundation Rnd: 7{7-11} sts.

Rows 4 thru 71{95-119}: Repeat Rows 2 and 3, 34{46-58} times.

Commercial fishing boats in the harbor.

Row 72{96-120} (Joining row)**:** Turn; skip first st on last row, matching **right** sides of beginning ch and last row, insert hook in free loop of first beginning ch and in Back Loop Only of next st on last row, YO and draw through all loops on hook, ★ insert hook in next free loop of beginning ch and in Back Loop Only of next st on last row, YO and draw through all loops on hook; repeat from ★ across; finish off leaving a long end for sewing.

FINISHING

Thread yarn needle with end and weave through loose loops along top edge *(Photo E, page 62)*.

Gather **tightly** to close and secure ends. Attach pom-pom *(Figs. 4a-c, page 63)* if desired.

BRAIDS

COMPLEX

Shopping List

Yarn

(Medium Weight) MEDIUM 4

[4 ounces, 203 yards (113 grams, 186 meters) per skein]:

☐ 1{2-2} skein(s)

Crochet Hook

☐ Size K (6.5 mm) **or** size needed for gauge

Additional Supplies

☐ Locking stitch markers - 11{13-15} Color A and 10{12-14} Color B

☐ Yarn needle

☐ Pom-pom (optional)

SIZE INFORMATION

Fits head circumference:

Small - 16-18" (40.5-45.5 cm)

Medium - 18½-20½" (47-52 cm)

Large - 21-23" (53.5-58.5 cm)

Size Note: For ease in following the pattern, we have printed the instructions for each size in a different color:

size Small in Blue

size Medium in Pink

size Large in Green

Instructions in Black apply to all sizes.

GAUGE INFORMATION

14 sts and 20 rows = 3½" (9 cm)

Gauge Swatch: 3½" (9 cm) square

Ch 15 **tightly**, pull last ch completely closed.

Row 1 (Right side)**:** Working in top loops of beginning ch ***(Fig. 1, page 61)***, slip st in second ch from hook and each ch across; ch 1, pull ch closed: 14 sts.

Rows 2-20: Turn; working in Back Loops Only ***(Fig. 3, page 61)***, slip st in each st across; ch 1, pull ch closed. Finish off.

BRAID STRIP

From The Top Down

DIVIDER ROWS

Ch 35{41-48} **tightly**, pull last ch completely closed.

Row 1 (Right side)**:** Working in top loops of beginning ch ***(Fig. 1, page 61)***, slip st in second ch from hook and each ch across; ch 1, pull ch closed: 34{40-47} sts.

Row 2 (Foundation Row - WS)**:** Turn; working in Back Loops Only ***(Fig. 3, page 61)***, slip st in first 10{12-15} sts, inverted slip st in last 24{28-32} sts ***(see Six Types of Slip Stitches, page 7);*** ch 1, pull ch closed.

BRAID UNIT 1 - Row 3 (RS)**:** Turn; slip st in Front Loop Only of first 4 sts; ch 1, place Color A marker in front loop of ch just made.

Row 4 (WS)**:** Turn; slip st in Back Loop Only of each st across; ch 1, pull ch closed.

BRAID UNIT 2 - Row 5 (RS)**:** Turn; slip st in Back Loop Only of first 4 sts, ch 1, push marker to **wrong** side; working in Foundation Row, slip st in Front Loop Only of next 4 sts; ch 1, place Color A marker in front loop of ch just made: 8 slip sts and 1 ch.

Row 6 (WS)**:** Turn; working in Back Loops Only, slip st in first 4 sts, slip st in next ch and in next 4 sts; ch 1, pull ch closed: 9 slip sts.

Row 7 (RS)**:** Turn; slip st in Back Loop Only of first 9 sts; ch 1, place Color A marker in front loop of ch just made.

Row 8 (WS)**:** Turn; slip st in Back Loop Only of each st across; ch 1, pull ch closed.

BRAID UNIT 3 - Row 9 (RS)**:** Turn; slip st in Back Loop Only of first 9 sts, ch 1, push markers to **wrong** side; working in sts on Foundation Row, slip st in Front Loop Only of next 4 sts; ch 1, place Color A marker in front loop of ch just made: 13 slip sts and 1 ch.

Row 10 (WS)**:** Turn; working in Back Loops Only, slip st in first 4 sts, slip st in next ch and in next 5 sts; ch 1, place Color B marker in front loop of ch just made: 10 slip sts.

Row 11 (RS)**:** Turn; slip st in Back Loop Only of first 10 sts; ch 1, place Color A marker in front loop of ch just made.

Row 12 (WS)**:** Turn; slip st in Back Loop Only of each st across; ch 1, place Color B marker in front loop of ch just made.

BRAID UNIT 4 - Row 13 (RS)**:** Turn; slip st in Back Loop Only of first 10 sts, ch 1, push markers to **wrong** side; working in sts on Foundation Row, slip st in Front Loop Only of next 4 sts; ch 1, place Color A marker in front loop of ch just made: 14 slip sts and 1 ch.

Row 14 (WS)**:** Turn; working in Back Loops Only, slip st in first 4 sts, slip st in next ch and in next 5 sts; ch 1, place Color B marker in front loop of ch just made: 10 sts.

Row 15 (RS)**:** Turn; slip st in Back Loop Only of first 10 sts; ch 1, place Color A marker in front loop of ch just made.

Row 16 (WS)**:** Turn; slip st in Back Loop Only of each st across; ch 1, place Color B marker in front loop of ch just made.

BRAID UNITS 5 THRU 6{7-8} - Rows 17 thru 24{28-32}: Repeat Rows 13-16, 2{3-4} times **more**.

CUFF - Row 25{29-33} (RS)**:** Turn; slip st in Back Loop Only of first 10 sts, ch 1, push markers to **wrong** side; working in sts on Foundation Row, slip st in Back Loop Only of last 10{12-15} sts; ch 1, pull ch closed: 20{22-25} slip sts and 1 ch.

Row 26{30-34} (WS)**:** Turn; working in Back Loops Only, slip st in first 10{12-15} sts, slip st in next ch and in next 5 sts; ch 1, place Color B marker in front loop of ch just made: 16{18-21} slip sts.

Row 27{31-35} (RS)**:** Turn; slip st in Back Loop Only of each st across; ch 1, pull ch closed.

Row 28{32-36} (WS)**:** Turn; slip st in Back Loop Only of each st across; ch 1, place Color B marker in front loop of ch just made.

Row 29{33-37} (RS)**:** Turn; slip st in Back Loop Only of each st across; ch 1, pull ch closed.

Along the working edges of the Braid Units and Cuff there should be 40 available sps. This is the new Foundation Row.

From The Bottom Up

CUFF - Row 30{34-38} (WS)**:** Turn; slip st in Back Loop Only of first 11{13-16} sts; working in **front** of previous rows, insert hook in **both** Color A marked loops below, YO and draw through all loops on hook, do **not** remove markers, slip st in Back Loop Only of next 5 sts across next Braid Unit; working in **front** of previous rows, pull Color B markers to the right, insert hook in **both** Color A marked loops below, YO and draw through all loops on hook, remove both Color A markers: 18{20 23} slip sts.

BRAID UNIT 6{7-8} - Row 31{35-39} (RS)**:** Turn; skip first st, slip st in Back Loop Only of next 5 sts, insert hook in **both** Color A marked loops behind work, YO and draw through all loops on hook, remove both markers: 6 slip sts.

BRAID UNIT 5{6-7} - Row 32{36-40} (WS)**:** Turn; skip first st, slip st in **both** loops of next 5 sts, keeping Color B markers to the right, slip st in Back Loop Only of next 5 sts on **next** Braid Unit, pull Color B markers to the right, insert hook in **both** Color A marked loops below, YO and draw through all loops on hook, remove markers: 11 slip sts.

Row 33{37-41} (RS)**:** Turn; skip first st, slip st in Back Loop Only of next 5 sts, insert hook in **both** Color B marked loops behind work, YO and draw through all loops on hook, remove markers: 6 slip sts.

NEXT 2{3-4} BRAID UNITS - Rows 34{38-42} thru 37{43-49}: Repeat Rows 32{36-40} and 33{37-41}, 2{3-4} time: 6 slip sts.

BRAID UNIT 2 - Row 38{44-50} (WS)**:** Turn; skip first st, slip st in **both** loops of next 5 sts, keeping Color B markers to the right, slip st in Back Loop Only of next 5 sts on **next** Braid Unit, pull Color B markers to the right, insert hook in Color A marked loop below, YO and draw through all loops on hook, remove marker: 11 slip sts.

Row 39{45-51} (RS)**:** Turn; slip st in Back Loop Only of next 5 sts, insert hook in **both** Color B marked loops behind work, YO and draw through all loops on hook, remove markers: 6 slip sts.

BRAID UNIT 1 - Row 40{46-52} (WS)**:** Turn; skip first st, slip st in **both** loops of next 5 sts, pull Color B markers to the right, slip st in Back Loop Only of last 4 sts on last Braid Unit; ch 1, pull ch closed: 9 slip sts.

Row 41{47-53} (RS)**:** Turn; slip st in Back Loop Only of first 4 sts, insert hook in **both** Color B marked loops behind work, YO and draw through all loops on hook, remove markers: 5 slip sts.

Row 42{48-54} (WS)**:** Turn; skip first st, slip st in **both** loops of last 4 sts; ch 1, pull ch closed.

Cascade waterfall through the rocks.

The sts across the top of each unit are the new Foundation Row. If you have made a mistake somewhere in the braid and you have a few more or less than 40{47-55} sts, don't tear it all out. You can skip or add a few sts in Row 43{49-55} to make up for it and it won't really show. Just make sure to work 34{40-47} sts in Row 43{49-55} to give you the correct number of sts for Row 44{50-56}.

Row 43{49-55} (RS)**:** Turn; working in Back Loops Only, slip st in first 4 sts, ★ slip st in first 4 sts on next Unit, skip last st on same Unit; repeat from ★ 4{5-6} times **more**, skip next st of Cuff, slip st in last 10{12-15} sts; ch 1, pull ch closed: 34{40-47} slip sts.

DIVIDER ROWS

Row 44{50-56} (WS)**:** Turn; slip st in Back Loop Only of first 10{12-15} sts, inverted slip st in each st across.

Row 45{51-57} (RS)**:** Ch 1, turn; pull turning ch closed, slip st in Front Loop Only of first 24{28-32} sts, slip st in Back Loop Only of each st across.

Row 46{52-58} (WS)**:** Ch 1, turn; pull turning ch closed, slip st in Back Loop Only of first 10{12-15} sts, slip st in **both** loops of each st across.

Braid Strip complete.

Row 47{53-59} (RS)**:** Ch 1, turn; pull turning ch closed, slip st in Back Loop Only of each st across.

Repeat Rows 2 thru 47{53-59}, 3{5-6} times; then Repeat Rows 2 thru 45{51-57} once **more**.

At end of last row, ch 1, pull ch closed. Remove loop from hook and place on locking st marker.

The unstretched rectangle should measure 8" x 13" (20.5 cm x 33 cm) for size Small, 10" x 18" (25.5 cm x 45.5 cm) for size Medium and 12" x 20½" (30.5 cm x 52 cm) for size Large. Add or subtract rows to achieve a perfect fit, ending by working Row 45{51-57}.

FINISHING

See Finishing, page 62.

YARN INFORMATION

Each Hat in this book was made using Medium Weight Yarn. Any brand of Medium Weight Yarn may be used. It is best to refer to the yardage/meters when determining how many balls or skeins to purchase. Remember, to arrive at the finished size, it is the GAUGE/TENSION that is important, not the brand of yarn.

For your convenience, listed in the following columns are the specific yarns used to create our photography models. Because yarn manufacturers make frequent changes to their product lines, you may sometimes find it necessary to use a substitute yarn or to search for the discontinued product at alternate suppliers (locally or online).

SIMPLE SLIP STITCH
Caron® Simply Soft® Tweeds™
23001 Off White Tweeds
#23002 Gray Heather Tweed

BOBBLES HAT
Red Heart® Soft®
#9770 Rose Blush
#9623 Spearmint

CHECKERED SLOUCH HAT
Caron® Simply Soft® Tweeds™
#23002 Gray Heather Tweed

BOBBLES & RIDGES
Lion Brand® New Basic 175™
#151 Slate

BASIC CABLES
Red Heart® Soft®
#4360 Cocoa
Premier® Anti-Pilling Everyday® Worsted
#100-52 Chinchilla

CABLES & BOBBLES
Red Heart® Soft®
#9623 Spearmint

CABLES IN THE ROUND
Premier® Anti-Pilling Everyday® Worsted
#100-52 Chinchilla
Red Heart® Soft®
#9770 Rose Blush

BRAIDS
Premier® Anti-Pilling Everyday® Worsted
#100-51 Spa

GENERAL INSTRUCTIONS

ABBREVIATIONS

ch(s)	chain(s)
cm	centimeters
hdc	half double crochet(s)
mm	millimeters
RS	right side
Rnd(s)	Round(s)
sc	single crochet(s)
sp(s)	space(s)
st(s)	stitch(es)
tr	treble crochet(s)
WS	wrong side
YO	yarn over

SYMBOLS & TERMS

★ — work instructions following ★ as many **more** times as indicated in addition to the first time.

† to † — work all instructions from first † to second † as many times as specified.

( ) or **[ ]** — work enclosed instructions **as many** times as specified by the number immediately following **or** work all enclosed instructions in the stitch or space indicated **or** contains explanatory remarks.

colon (:) — the number(s) given after a colon at the end of a row or round denote(s) the number of stitches and spaces you should have on that row or round.

GAUGE

Exact gauge is essential for proper size. Before beginning your hat, make the sample swatch given in the individual instructions in the yarn and hook specified. After completing the swatch, measure it, counting your stitches and rows carefully. If your swatch is larger or smaller than specified, make another, changing hook size to get the correct gauge. Keep trying until you find the size hook that will give you the specified gauge.

Yarn Weight Symbol & Names	LACE 0	SUPER FINE 1	FINE 2	LIGHT 3	MEDIUM 4	BULKY 5	SUPER BULKY 6	JUMBO 7
Type of Yarns in Category	Fingering, size 10 crochet thread	Sock, Fingering, Baby	Sport, Baby	DK, Light Worsted	Worsted, Afghan, Aran	Chunky, Craft, Rug	Super Bulky, Roving	Jumbo, Roving
Crochet Gauge* Ranges in Single Crochet to 4" (10 cm)	32-42 sts**	21-32 sts	16-20 sts	12-17 sts	11-14 sts	8-11 sts	6-9 sts	5 sts and fewer
Advised Hook Size Range	Steel*** 6 to 8, Regular hook B-1	B-1 to E-4	E-4 to 7	7 to I-9	I-9 to K-10½	K-10½ to M/N-13	M/N-13 to Q	Q and larger

*GUIDELINES ONLY: The chart above reflects the most commonly used gauges and hook sizes for specific yarn categories.

** Lace weight yarns are usually crocheted with larger hooks to create lacy openwork patterns. Accordingly, a gauge range is difficult to determine. Always follow the gauge stated in your pattern.

*** Steel crochet hooks are sized differently from regular hooks–the higher the number, the smaller the hook, which is the reverse of regular hook sizing.

CROCHET TERMINOLOGY

UNITED STATES		INTERNATIONAL
slip stitch (slip st)	=	single crochet (sc)
single crochet (sc)	=	double crochet (dc)
half double crochet (hdc)	=	half treble crochet (htr)
double crochet (dc)	=	treble crochet (tr)
treble crochet (tr)	=	double treble crochet (dtr)
double treble crochet (dtr)	=	triple treble crochet (ttr)
triple treble crochet (tr tr)	=	quadruple treble crochet (qtr)
skip	=	miss

ZEROS

To consolidate the length of an involved pattern, zeros are sometimes used so that all sizes can be combined. For example, repeat from ★ 0{1-1} time(s) **more** means the first size would not repeat from ★ and the second and third sizes would repeat from ★ once.

TOP LOOPS OF A CHAIN

Work only in loops indicated by arrow *(Fig. 1)*.

Fig. 1

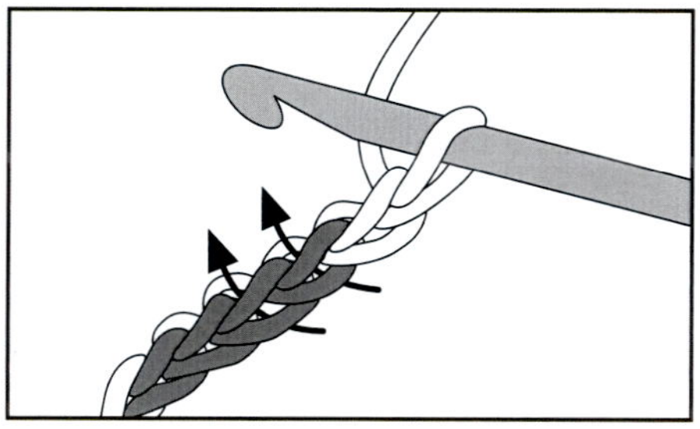

FREE LOOPS OF A CHAIN

When instructed to work in free loops of a chain, work in loop indicated by arrow *(Fig. 2)*.

Fig. 2

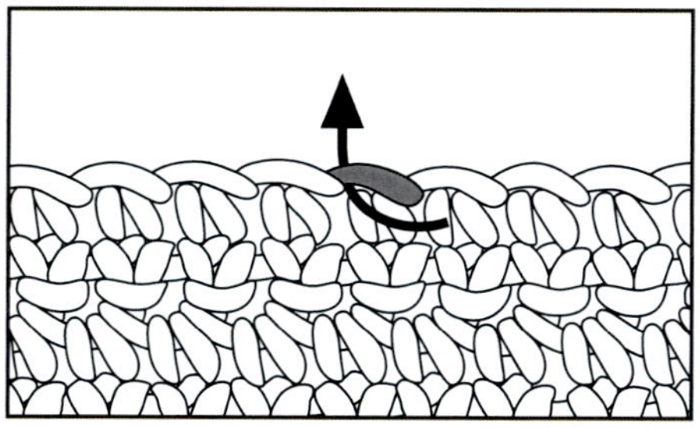

BACK OR FRONT LOOP ONLY

Work only in loop(s) indicated by arrow *(Fig. 3)*.

Fig. 3

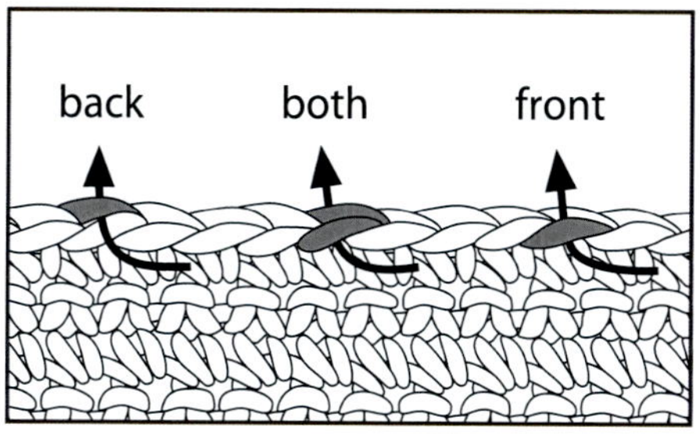

■□□□ **BASIC**	Projects using basic stitches. May include basic increases and decreases.
■■□□ **EASY**	Projects may include simple stitch patterns, color work, and/or shaping.
■■■□ **INTERMEDIATE**	Projects may include involved stitch patterns, color work, and/or shaping.
■■■■ **COMPLEX**	Projects may include complex stitch patterns, color work, and/or shaping using a variety of techniques and stitches simultaneously.

CROCHET HOOKS																
U.S.	B-1	C-2	D-3	E-4	F-5	G-6	7	H-8	I-9	J-10	K-10½	L-11	M/N-13	N/P-15	P/Q	Q	S
Metric - mm	2.25	2.75	3.25	3.5	3.75	4	4.5	5	5.5	6	6.5	8	9	10	15	16	19

FINISHING

Lay the rectangle flat with the st marker at the upper right corner and the tail of the foundation ch at the bottom right corner *(Photo A)*.

Photo A

SEAM

Fold the rectangle in half with **right** sides of last row and beginning ch together *(Photo B)* and beginning ch on top.

Photo B

Remove marker and place loop on hook; insert opposite end of hook in free loop of first beginning ch *(Photo C)*, draw loop through beginning ch *(Photo D)*.

Photo C

Photo D

You may find it easier to insert your hook in the free loop of the beginning ch *(Fig. 2, page 61)*, then place marked loop on hook, YO and draw through beginning ch.

To finish the seam, ★ slip st **tightly** through **both** edges by inserting your hook first through bottom free loops of next ch and then through Back Loop Only of next slip st on last row, YO and draw through all loops on hook; repeat from ★ across; finish off.

The side of the hat is now closed. Notice that when the hat is laying relaxed on a table the seam is visible, but when you stretch the hat out a little bit, the seam becomes invisible.

CLOSING TOP OF HAT

Cut a 12" (30.5 cm) length of yarn. Thread yarn needle with end and weave through loose loops along top edge *(Photo E)*.

Photo E

POM-POM

Cut a piece of cardboard 3" (7.5 cm) wide and as long as you want the diameter of your finished pom-pom to be.

Wind the yarn around the cardboard until it is approximately ½" (12 mm) thick in the middle ***(Fig. 4a)***. Carefully slip the yarn off the cardboard and firmly tie an 18" (45.5 cm) length of yarn around the middle ***(Fig. 4b)***. Leave yarn ends long enough to attach the pom-pom. Cut the loops on both ends and trim the pom-pom into a smooth ball ***(Fig. 4c)***.

Fig. 4a

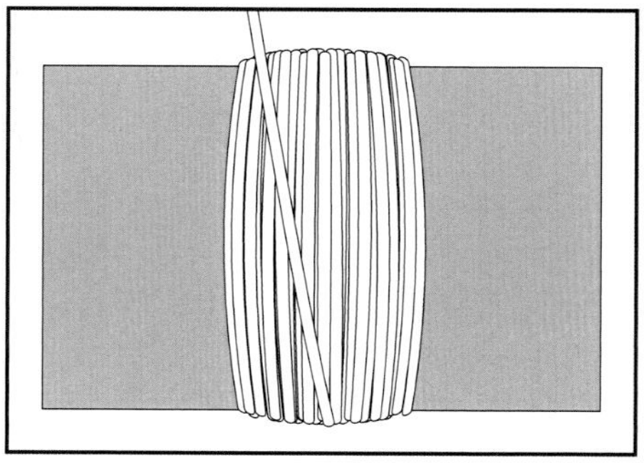

Fig. 4b

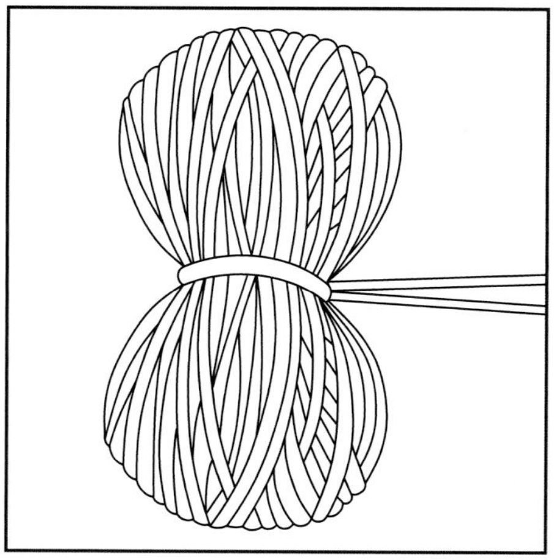

Fig. 4c

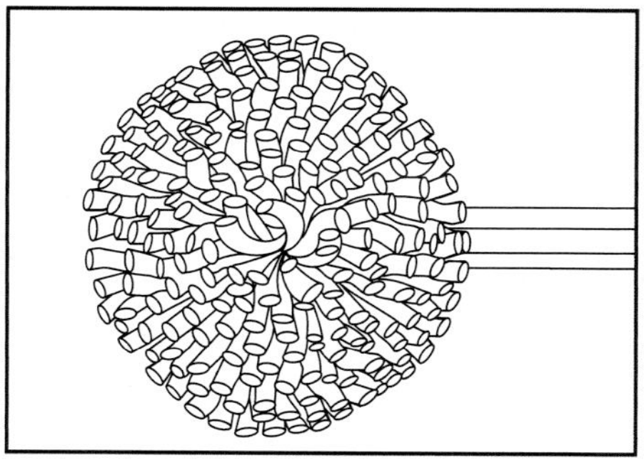

Library of Congress Control Number: 2019952238

Production Team: Project Manager - Linda A. Daley; Instructional/ Technical Editors - Joan Beebe and Sarah J. Green; Graphic Artist - Angela Ormsby Stark; Photo Stylist - Lori Wenger; and Photographer - Jason Masters.

Made in U.S.A.